Woman Rising

Melissa George

BookLeaf Publishing

India | USA | UK

Presentation by *BookLeaf Publishing*

Web: www.bookleafpub.com

E-mail: info@bookleafpub.com

ISBN: 9789363314566

First edition 2024

"Woman Rising" is dedicated to my Dad.

My original knight in shining armor.

The man who taught me to live big and love even bigger.

The one who always believed in me even if I didn't.

He taught me to look people in the eyes and to always have a firm handshake. Especially when shaking a man's hand.

He'd say, "Never back down and show 'em who's boss Missy doll."

When my dad passed he gave me the greatest gift anyone could ever give.

The gift of awareness and the courage to follow my dreams.

He always said I should be a writer.

Well, here I am daddy.

I'll always be your little girl

To My Lover

To the one whose touch I love.

Lightly upon my skin, your fingertips play a sweet song that lingers long after we've kissed goodbye.

A melody that hums to me softly all day long.

A far away dream of how golden that moment will be when I can hold you once again.

Unrequited Love

He stood there with my hand inside of his and said, " You're too good for him. His feet are firmly planted on Earth and you are stardust in the ether and never shall those two planes meet."

The most beautiful words I have ever heard.

Words I shall never forget.

Words that will reverberate in the chambers of my soul until time and energy no longer exist.

But words are just words.

The heartache of unrequited love.

Reconciliation

I'm sorry I broke your heart. I didn't respect you as I should. I didn't listen to you or love you the way you deserved to be loved. You're worthy of so much more. If only you could see that.

I'm sorry that I left you out in the cold time and time again. You deserve so much better in this lifetime. We seem to have this love-hate relationship. When we love, fuck do we love big and deep but oh God when we hate, hell hath no fury like a woman scorned.

My tongue is like a serpent, filled with venom with every word I speak to you. Sometimes taking pleasure in your pain. Most times actually. Relentless with my criticism. Making you feel such shame and guilt, never allowing you to move on from the past.

But then I come in with the I'm sorry baby. It'll be better this time. I promise. Until I do it again. And I always do. You know I do. You just keep coming back for more. Over and over again. Never learning your lesson.

I have you under my spell. I'm no good for you
baby. You should probably break up with me.
You know you should but you know you never
will. Besides, how do you break up with the
person in the mirror?

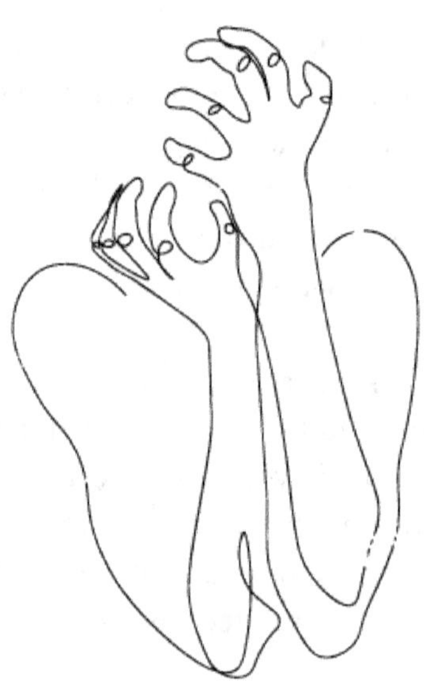

4

She Didn't Know

She was given her name.

She was told what God she would pray to.

She was told who and what was bad and who and what was good.

She was even told what made her bad and what made her good.

She was told what to say, what to wear and how to act.

She was told she was over dramatic because she felt so much and so big.

She was told "nice girls" are always polite even when she felt that her boundaries had been crossed.

She was told not to look mean and she should smile more often even when she didn't want to.

She was told she was too much when she had to fight for her voice to be heard.

She was told a story of a thousand lies.

She didn't know she could edit and do a rewrite
in the middle of the book.

She didn't know she could write her own story.

Until one day she did.

One Glance

All it took was one shared glance from across a crowded room and she knew she had found home.

The Mirror

The mirror says, " I hate the way your stomach looks. It's too big and flabby and one side stretches out further than the other."

The mirror says, "I hate your feet. They're chunky and wide and your toes are too stubby. You have Fred Flinstone feet."

The mirror says, "I hate your legs. Your right calf is smaller than the left and your thighs are too fat. No wonder why they called you thunder thighs when you were younger."

The mirror says, "I hate your breasts. They're too big and uneven. They're saggy and have

ugly stretch marks. They have always been a
source of shame and discomfort."

The mirror says, "I hate your hands. They are
not delicate and your fingers are not long and
thin. They are certainly not piano-playing hands.
You always wanted to play the piano, didn't
you?"

My body says, "I love and give thanks to your
stomach. It has held the precious life that you
have created. It's stretched out further on one
side because that's where your baby boy's bum
stuck out. Do you not remember the delight and
laughter you had because of that? Do you not
remember rubbing your belly to give comfort
when he was restless and stirring?"

My body says, " I love and give thanks to your
feet. They have helped you to walk miles and
miles. Do you not remember all the adventures
and wondrous places they have taken you?"

My body says, "I love and give thanks to your
legs. They are strong and sturdy. Do you not
remember how they held you up in the toughest
of times even when you wanted to fall?"

My body says, "I love and give thanks to your breasts. They are soft and supple. They give nourishment for a most delicate life. Do you not remember the peace you felt as your baby's head rested upon them as he slept?"

My body says, " I love and give thanks to your hands. They have caressed the cheek of your lover and have given you the ability to create the enchantment of your imagination to paper. Do you not remember the power of your love and creation?"

My body says, "I love and give thanks to the sublime beauty that is you."

Falling

Sometimes love can hurt.
There's a reason why they call it falling in love.
I'm falling hard.
I pray that you can catch me.

Stripped Away

She stripped away her guilt for the things she felt she had done wrong.

She stripped away her shame for embracing her sexuality and taking pleasure in it.

She stripped away the judgment she perceived others had of her.

She stripped away the repulsion she felt when looking in the mirror.

She stripped away the barbed wire fence that surrounded her heart.

She stripped away the pain from the past and the fear for the future.

She stripped away every story that wasn't true and every lie she was ever told.

She stripped away everything that no longer served her until she stood there naked and raw embracing all of her power and divine exquisiteness.

Sacred Union

I want to get lost inside the heavenly cosmos of
your eyes.

One look can express more than a thousand
encyclopedias and the most eloquent musings of
all the mystics and poets.

I want to fall into your arms until our bodies
melt together and our hearts flow in rhythm like
the beating of a drum.

Ba-bump, Ba-bump, Ba-bump

They say there is nothing more divine than when
we connect to our breath.

Connecting to our breath is to experience the
purest essence of God's soul.

I want to breathe in God's soul with you.

I want to feel your lips glide across my neck
while your fingertips gently caress my body like
the artist who paints soft strokes of color upon
the canvas.

I want to open my body to you like the delicate petals of a rose on a cool dewy morning in Spring.

I want time to stand still while we worship the sacred union of our love until we mend the scars of past lovers and the sins of our heart.

Be Still

Be still my aching heart.
You have no bones yet you are broken.
Drowning in heartache feeling abandoned and
lonely.
Tainted by the betrayal of love gone by and the
repression of what is true and what is not.

Be still my lover.
Be kind to me.
My heart sits trapped in a locked box made of
glass longing for the box to be shattered so it can
love and be loved once more.
It fears the agony of rejection and even the
beauty of what could be.
For it knows too well how quickly love can be
taken away.

Be still the one I love.
Please be patient with me and I shall place my
weary heart into your gentle open hands.
I ask that you treat it with care and love it the
way that it is worthy to be loved.
My heart loves deeply with passion and will be
forever true.

Be still my mending heart.
Your day will come soon beloved.
Love yourself like you would love another and
love shall find you once again.

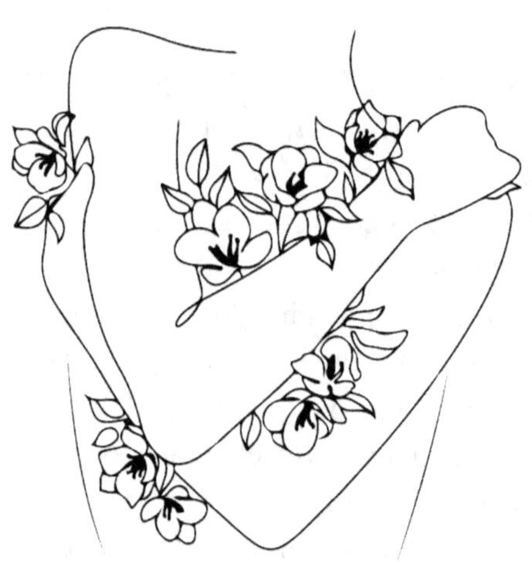

House on the Corner

My repression lives on the corner of guilt and
shame.
It's the biggest house on the block with a shiny
new car sitting in the driveway.
My mama's name is sexuality.
My daddy's name is rage.
They came together and built this home with
cracks in the stone foundation adorned with a
torn and tattered straw roof on top.

Mama likes to rock in her rocking chair.
She sits outside on the big front porch wearing
her skimpy negligee.
All the neighbors point and stare but mama
doesn't mind.
She smokes their cares away.

Daddy's in the garage angry and bitter waiting
for better days.
Always wanting, always wishing but always too
afraid to take the first step.
His mantra seems to be, maybe one day…
But daddy, what if one day never comes?

The birds sing a distant love song that they no
longer hear.
Drowned out by fear and loathing with a
sprinkle of lust for another and addiction as the
cherry on top.

Untitled and Unfinished

Your body is my church where I meet God and
lie down to pray.

Your mind is a vast wonderland begging to be
explored.

Your eyes hold all the wisdom my soul ever
needs to know.

Your voice speaks this perfectly orchestrated
truth that sends shivers down to the base of my
spine.

Your hands envelop mine until I don't know
where I end and you begin.

When you whisper my name I hold my breath so
you can't hear me sigh with desire.

When your lips meet mine electricity moves
down my body and grounds me like the ancient
Redwoods that are rooted deep within the Earth.

You…

Promise Me

Promise me that you'll love me madly and
deeply forever until the end of time.

Promise me you'll be patient with me even when
it's hard. Especially when I push you away.

Promise me you'll envelop me in your warm
embrace softly wiping my tears away when I'm
overcome with sadness.

Promise me you'll always say I love you and
kiss me goodnight, even when you're mad.

Promise me we'll stay up all night making love
and reading poetry to each other while lying
next to the fire.

Promise me you'll treat my heart tenderly for it
is tired and weary.

Promise me we'll laugh so hard that tears run
from our eyes down our smiling cheeks.

Promise me you'll always look at me like the
first time you realized you were crazy in love
with me and wanted us to be together lifetime
after lifetime.

Promise me you won't let me be the one that got
away.

Ways to Make Your Daughter Small

Tell her things like…

You should smile more. You don't want people to think you're a bitch.

You have such a pretty face. Don't cover it with your hair.

Don't be so dramatic. It's not that big of a deal.

Boys will be boys...

You'll be fine. Rub some dirt on it. It builds character.

"Good girls" are polite and always do what
they're told.

You'll get over it. Suck it up.

Stand up for yourself but don't be too pushy
about it.

If he's mean to you it just means he likes you.

Shower Thoughts and Other Epiphanies

Realizing that when you meet someone and you have this mutual physical attraction and you stimulate each other intellectually but he's kinda' arrogant and borderline narcissistic and that you simultaneously want to fight with him and fuck him is toxic as fuck. Yeah girl. Run the fuck away. Quickly.

What are the meaning of words and who made them up? Like who says that the name for an apple is named an apple? If I lived in the middle of the woods with other people and we decided that an apple was called a car then it would be a car. Who says that that would be a made up language if it was our language? It would be real to us.

Reality isn't real. Reality is only our perception and time is not linear.

Why do I still smell down there? Like what the fuck? I take a damn shower every day. Sometimes twice a day. I feel like that's not normal. Maybe I need to go to the doctors.

Fuck me. I need to leave him. How am I going to tell him after all these years I want a divorce?

Huh, dogs feet really do smell like Fritos. I wonder why.

Waterproof mascara is fake news. My tears are water and my mascara runs every time I cry.

Fuck me I'm so sexed up. I totally need some amazing mind blowing sex. I need it like yesterday. And today. And tomorrow...

Every dreamer needs a doer and every doer needs a dream to believe in. Shit. That's good. I need to write that down.

I think I'm gonna run away to a little cabin in the forest and become this reclusive mysterious witchy woman who writes poetry all day and makes love to an occasional lover in her moon garden under the glow of the full moon. I'll definitely need an army of black cats and a dog to go hiking in the woods with. That sounds perfect and dreamy. Fuck yeah. I'm totally doing that.

God, I'm so stupid. There were like a million red flags. How did I not see it? Fuck, I'm so dumb. That sucks cause I feel like the sex would've been amazing. Men suck sometimes. Asshole.

Women whose periods are synched to the full moon or the new moon are bad ass bitches.

God, I'm so lonely. So unbelievably lonely. I think I miss hugs the most.

I think I want to learn how to play the cello. Maybe I can become the next Yo-Yo Ma. My stage name could be Mo-Mo Lissa. I dig it. I'm so gonna learn how to play the cello.

The next dog or cat I get I'm totally naming it Garbanzo. But I'll make everyone say its name in this super exaggerated Italian accent rolling the R's like Garrrrrrbanzo. Or maybe I'll name it Clementine Paddleford. That would be fucking amazing.

I feel like I think about sex way too much. Well, maybe if I had some good sex I'd stop thinking about it. Ugh. There I go again.

Best Served Cold

You played with my mind never giving it a
second thought.
You so callously shut me down when I tried to
speak my truth.
You broke my heart when you walked out the
door leaving me to pick up the pieces.
You may think you've moved on but you'll
quickly realize that I was the first place prize
you know you'll never win.
You'll want to sleep forever because your
dreams will be the only place you'll see me.
You'll hope to catch a glimpse of me around
every corner you turn but you won't.
Every woman you ever kiss you'll be thinking of
how sweet my lips were pressed against yours.
Every woman that ever lies in your bed you'll be
wishing was me.
You'll be begging the Universe to bring me back
to you but it never will.
The memory of me will haunt you until your
very last breath.
They say revenge is a dish best served cold.
Baby, mine will be served on a bed of ice.

The Princesses and The Tree

Let me tell you the tale of a gaggle of princesses and one lonely tree.

Once there was a little girl who at the age of seven wanted nothing more than to be a princess in the school play. Sadly though, the teacher deemed her to take the role of the lonely tree.

The little girl would watch the princesses from across the stage whispering and giggling as if they knew some glorious secret. She longed to whisper and giggle and know their secret too. But alas the little girl was not a princess, only a tree.

Many years passed and the little girl grew up. She got lost in being a wife and a mother. She remembered that little girl of long ago who so desperately wanted to be seen, who wanted to belong. A little girl who terribly wanted to be a princess.

Then she thought, "Fuck being a princess. A princess always needs to be saved. I don't need saving." In that moment she realized that maybe she was a tree.

A tree stands tall and proud rooted in the wisdom of Mother Gaia. A tree is a home for the birds and the animals of the forest. In the summer when her leaves are lush and green she is a shaded place for the weary traveler.

In the fall she stands with her beauty in vibrant colors of reds, oranges, purples and yellows. She is the epitome of wabi-sabi. Beautifully perfect in her imperfection as she sheds her leaves to welcome winter's morn.

The death of the old only to be reborn once again in the spring when her leaves begin to wake and sprout from their slumber and her budding flowers bloom fragrantly.

She is a tree.
She stands tall and is rooted in the Earth as her branches reach high towards the Divine.
She is *strong*.
She is *resilient*.
She is *wise*.
She is *beautiful*.

She has died and been reborn time and time
again yet she is still here.

She is still love.

She too is beautifully perfect in her imperfection
and chooses to no longer apologize for it but
embrace it with all of her being. She has
awakened and surrendered to who she truly is.

She didn't need anyone to save her because she
had the power to save herself all along.
And she did.

The Dreamer Within

She was the little girl with her head in the clouds
and her nose in a book.

Always dreaming of far-off places that one day
she would explore.

Her heart still innocent not yet burdened by
worries or fear.

One day she would dance and twirl in her moon
garden and swing on her swing in the glow of
the full moon.

She dreamed of a love that was pure and true.
The kind of love that fairytales were made of.

Until one day, she got in trouble and had to stay
after school.
Her teacher drove her home but not before he
showed her where he lived.

The little girl no longer dreams of love or
faraway places.
Dancing in her moon garden became a distant
memory.

She grew her hair long so she could cover her
face.
Maybe if she couldn't see the world, the world
wouldn't see her.

She ate in the middle of the night to gain weight.
Maybe if she was fat no one would like her.

She slouched her shoulders in shame hoping no
one would notice her developing breasts that
were quickly growing.

She did everything in her power to keep small
and fade away until one day she was never seen
again.

Lifetime After Lifetime

If I lived a thousand lifetimes I would find you a
thousand times.

I would move mountains and part seas.

I would travel to the ends of the Universe just to
look into your eyes and hold you in my arms.

I'd do anything and everything for just one
fleeting moment in time with you.

Sinking Ship

Every night she would come home and take a long shower. She would blast the music to muffle the sound of her crying. If her husband walked in the water would hide her tears.

She spent hours locked in the bathroom, her only refuge from the outside world. Sobbing quietly into the plush turkish cotton towels until she collapsed onto the floor from exhaustion. The floor quickly became her friend as she soon found comfort in its cool hard tiles. The gray shag mat became a soothing and restful place to lay her aching head. She came to know every crack and chip in the fleshy pink tiles. She noticed every discoloration and missing piece of

grout. It reminded her of the cracked and
missing pieces of her heart.

How could she tell the man she had been with
more than half her life, a man she had spent
more time with than with herself, that she could
no longer go on? She knew she must leave. She
was more than tired. She was exhausted to the
depths of her soul.

Who was this person in the mirror looking back
at her? How long had those creases around her
eyes and mouth been there? When did those
lines in her forehead become so deep? She could
see them even when her brow wasn't furrowed.
When did she begin to look so tired and old?
When did her eyes become so sad? She no
longer knew who she was. Maybe she never did.

Fear erupted within her.
What would she say to him?
What would he say back?
What would her friends and family say?
How would she survive?
How could she walk away after so many years?
Her body shuttered with guilt and shame.

She knew the ship was sinking and that she
needed to swim back to shore to regain her

strength. Maybe then she could swim back to save her family. She quickly learned though that sometimes love isn't enough and the only person that can save us is ourself.

Woman Rising

37

I am woman rising.
The perfect *balance* of divine feminine and
masculine energy.
I am the nurturer.
I am the protector.
Unconditional love and *creation* flow through
me effortlessly and with ease.

I am divine beauty.
I am the muse that inspires timeless love songs
and words for the poet.

I am the Empress.
I sit in abundance.
I do not chase.
I attract.
Anything I want wants me more.
Anyone I desire desires me more.

I am in love with the Universe and the Universe
is in love with me *for we are one in the same.*
I follow the *signs* and *synchronicities* of life and
take great delight in dancing with the Universe.

I listen to my heart.
That is where my intuition lies and when I do,
the Divine always rewards.
Everything I seek is within.

I sit in *gratitude* and *appreciation* for all that I
have and all that I don't.
I am worthy and deserving of love that is true.
What is meant for me will always find me.

I am loving and kind.
I am raw and vulnerable.
I am real.

I am in love with myself completely and no
longer have judgment for who I am.
I speak my *truth* and sit in *authenticity* so that I
may hold space for others to do the same.
I am *open* and *receptive* to the magical unfolding
of the Universe.

*I am the ultimate alchemist of all my dreams and
desires.*

Awakened Souls

I'll know by his eyes.
He'll know by my smile.
It'll be this moment where it feels serene and
familiar like the comfort of home.
He'll say, "Have we met before? I feel like I
know you."
I'll say, "Maybe we did in another life."
Time will cease to exist as our souls awaken and
remember that we were destined to be together
in this one.

Letter of Apology

Dear Seven Year Old Me,

    I sit here in your adult body reflecting upon all our many years together. I've realized how much pain I have inflicted on you. I told you that you were different and that no one liked you. I told you that you were fat and that boys don't like girls who are fat. I told you that you were ugly and that you weren't as pretty as all the other girls. I made you repress your sexuality. Especially if you found it to be pleasurable or exciting. I told you that you were dumb and an eternal fuck up. I continually told you that you were a disappointment to your parents and how you always let them down. I kept you small even though you were meant to shine. As you grew older I told you that you were a terrible wife and you fucked up being a mother even more. I constantly threw every single perceived mistake in your face.

My biggest transgression is that I did not allow you to just be you. I taught you at a very young age that in order to survive you must wear masks. You wore a different mask for each person in your life. I taught you to be a mirror in order to reflect what was around you. If you were just like them then they'd feel comfortable which made you feel safe. It protected you from pain and heartache, from being rejected, abandoned and made fun of. I thought I was doing the right thing. I thought I was keeping you from harm's way but I was deeply and sadly mistaken. It was all a lie. By keeping you trapped within this box I rejected the beautiful divine person that you are. It's time now for you to put the masks in the closet and shatter the mirror. I love and am proud of the woman you are right now at this very moment in time. Please forgive me my love.

- Shame

Slow Way Home

I feel as if I'm floating in the ether waiting for directions.
There's this aching in my heart that's longing for ease.
I am lonely and homesick with no place to call home.
I fantasize about my perfect home and daydream of what it will look like.
I read books on aesthetics and feng shui.
I scour all the home magazines searching for just the right furniture and paint color to match.
I'm determined to finally make this home flawless in every way.
This home will feel like love.
The kind of love you get from your beloved childhood dog when they snuggle close at night while lying in bed.
It will be a home that feels safe and secure like the warmth of my mother's embrace.
My home will always be filled with laughter that makes my eyes cry and where my cheeks hurt from smiling.
A home that has a gentle and welcoming kindness that touches the very depths of my soul.

In this home I'll sing at the top of my lungs to
my favorite songs.
I'll twirl and dance in the kitchen as I bake the
most delectable homemade pies and cookies.
I searched and I searched, traveling the world
looking for that one magnificent piece of heaven
to finally call my home but I could never seem
to find just the right fit.
'Til one day I realized I had never left home.
Home is wherever I am.
Home is where the heart is and my heart is
within me.

Melissa's Song

I love Melissa
Melissa's my little girl
I love Melissa
From the tip of her toes to her curls

I love Melissa
I love her oh so much
It's time to go to bed now
It's time to go to sleep